IMAGES
of America

DELAWARE WATER GAP
THE STROUDSBURGS
AND THE POCONOS

November, 1995

To Lorraine Long,

Best wishes!

Sally Freedman

IMAGES of America

DELAWARE WATER GAP THE STROUDSBURGS AND THE POCONOS

By
Sally A. Freedman

ARCADIA

First published 1995
Copyright © Sally A. Freedman, 1995

ISBN 0-7524-0100-9

Published by Arcadia Publishing,
an imprint of the Chalford Publishing Corporation
One Washington Center, Dover, New Hampshire 03820
Printed in Great Britain

Library of Congress Cataloging-in-Publication Data applied for

Contents

Introduction		7
1.	The Mountains and the River	9
2.	Delaware Water Gap	21
3.	The Resorts	31
4.	Getting There	41
5.	Stroudsburg	49
6.	East Stroudsburg	59
7.	The Mountain Towns	69
8.	Growing Up in the Poconos	79
9.	Making A Living	89
10.	Having Fun	99
11.	The Music Makers	109
12.	The Great Outdoors	117
Acknowledgments		128
References		128

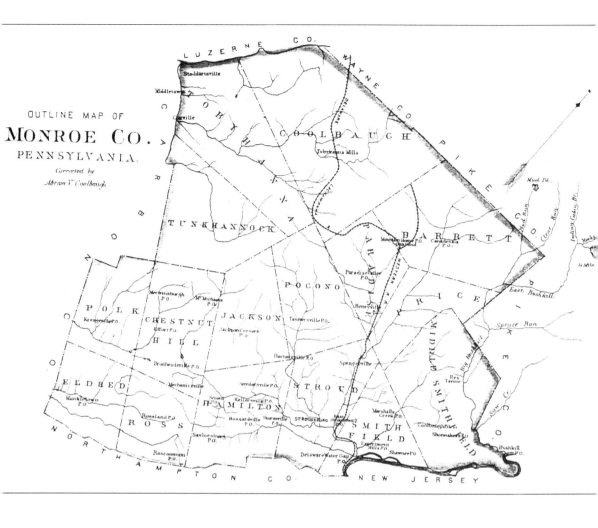

Introduction

In the northeastern section of Pennsylvania, along its Delaware River boundary, lies a series of rolling mountains at the edge of the Appalachian Plateau called the Poconos. Forested with oak, maple, beech, and hemlock trees and graced by bubbling streams, splashing waterfalls, and broad valleys, the mountains were the home of members of the Wolf clan of the Lenni Lenape nation when the man destined to be the first permanent white settler arrived in 1725 to look over the land.

Nicholas Depui, or Depuy, grandson of an early French Huguenot settler in a Dutch colony on the Hudson River, traveled from Esopus (now Kingston, New York) into New Jersey on the Old Mine Road, which had been built by the Dutch to mine copper near the Delaware River. Depui crossed the Delaware near the Kittatinny Mountain gap cut by the river, and entered the Lenape's Minisink Valley, a beautiful area he thought fit for farming. Two years later, he returned to negotiate with the Lenape for 3,000 acres of land there. He and his wife Wyntje built a home and grist mill, planted an apple orchard, and proceeded to produce wheat, cider, and a family of four sons and five daughters. The wheat and cider he took back to Esopus to sell each year.

Other settlers soon followed, among them the parents of a lad named Jacob Stroud, who lived with the Depuis as an apprentice until he was twenty-one and ended up marrying one of Depui's granddaughters, Elizabeth McDowell, in 1761. Stroud became the founder of the town of Stroudsburg, and he and Elizabeth produced twelve children of their own: nine sons and three daughters. A neighbor, Daniel Brodshead, founded East Stroudsburg, which was originally named Dansbury in his honor.

The peaceful life of the Poconos was disrupted by violent clashes with the Lenape clansmen after William Penn's son, Thomas, tricked them with a land deal known as the Walking Purchase of 1737. Until that year, the northern boundary of Bucks County in Penn's colony was just south of today's Doylestown. Thomas Penn, whose father was then deceased, got the Lenape to agree to sell as much land as a white man could mark off by walking northwestward for one and one-half days and then drawing a straight line to the Delaware River. Penn found a champion walker, Edward Marshall, who reached a point near today's Jim Thorpe. Then Penn drew his line, not straight east to the river but straight northeast, thus acquiring more than two thirds of present day Monroe County for pioneer settlers and infuriating the Lenape.

When the French and English went to war in 1754, the French stiffened the resolve of the Lenape to stay and drive off the Poconos settlers. Subsequent attacks led to the building of a chain of forts by the Penns; Fort Hamilton, near present Stroudsburg, was one of them. These were effective, but attacks continued through 1763 when the Indian Wars ended. Then peace returned briefly until the American Revolution began.

By 1769, Jacob Stroud had bought 300 acres of land and a grist mill west of Dansbury beside Brodhead's Creek, and settled down to operate the grist mill, a saw mill, a blacksmith shop, and a general store. He fought in the Revolution as captain of a volunteer company, moving up to the rank of colonel by the war's end. He was elected a delegate to the first Pennsylvania Constitutional Convention on July 8, 1776, and in 1781–83 was a representative in the Pennsylvania General Assembly. Stroud laid out lots for his town in 1799, but it was left to his son, Daniel, to lead the further development of Stroudsburg because Jacob was thrown from a buggy and killed in 1806.

In 1793, Antoine Dutot, a French plantation owner in Santo Domingo, fled a slave uprising and went to Philadelphia, where he accepted advice to travel up the Delaware River to the Gap. There he purchased a large tract of land and began to lay out a city. He built a dozen or so buildings, marked out a triangle of land for a market place, and named the town Dutotsburg. In 1800, a wagon road was built along the Delaware River past the Gap, and as early as 1820 visitors to the area were staying in Dutotsburg, rooming with local families so as to enjoy the scenery.

Dutot noted this and began building a small hotel overlooking the river in 1829. By 1832, though, he had run out of money, and sold the incomplete building to Samuel Snyder. Snyder enlarged and completed it as the Kittatinny House, Delaware Water Gap's first hotel. It accommodated twenty-five people, and was filled throughout its first season. Later owners continued to enlarge it, and by 1860 it accommodated 250 guests. The village of Dutotsburg was then called Delaware Water Gap.

It seems inevitable that the wild beauty of the Pocono Mountains, not far from Philadelphia and only six hours' journey from New York City by train, should have drawn city dwellers like a magnet to spend summer vacations in the area. By 1846, a passenger and mail stage coach stopped in Stroudsburg on the way to Milford from Easton three times a week. But it was the Delaware, Lackawanna and Western Railroad which in 1856 began transporting eastern city dwellers to the Poconos in droves. One writer said Delaware Water Gap was "the second largest inland resort town in the United States after the Civil War [ranking behind Saratoga Springs, New York], and its clientele were the upper classes of Philadelphia and New York." Its heyday ended with the coming of the automobile and the Depression. But some resorts remain, many modern hotels and condominiums have been built, and tourism is once more flourishing as the major industry of the Poconos.

One
The Mountain and the River

Pennsylvania's Delaware Water Gap, formed by the Delaware River as it cut through the Kittatinnys between Mount Minsi (Pennsylvania) and Mount Tammany (New Jersey) eons ago, has been a recreational beacon to urbanites of New York, New Jersey, and Philadelphia since the 1830s. Perhaps the best-known view of the Gap is this postcard scene, sent in the thousands over the years by summer visitors to friends back home. U.S. Highway 80 passes through the Gap today. The Appalachian Trail crosses the river nearby. The river and the Pocono Mountains together comprise what many easterners have felt is the perfect getaway from city life. (Monroe County Historical Association photograph.)

Robert Reading Depui, a descendent of the Pocono's first permanent settler, Nicholas Depui, built the original part of this house in Shawnee around 1785. (M.C.H.A. photograph.)

Antoine Dutot is said to have started the resort industry in the Poconos when he began building the first "boarding house" in 1829. But it was Samuel Snyder who completed the building and called it the Kittatinny House. Later owners made it into one of the nation's largest "grand hotels." (M.C.H.A. photograph.)

The Delaware Indians, or Lenni Lenape, called the upper river valley the Minisink. This view of the meandering river is looking north from the Gap's Winona Cliff. (M.C.H.A. photograph.)

Bucolic scenes of sheep fields and farmlands were a major drawing card for city dwellers. Businessmen brought their families to a favorite resort to spend the entire summer and joined them on weekends and brief holidays. (M.C.H.A. photograph.)

A glory of the Poconos is its many waterfalls. Chief among them is Bushkill Falls, called "the Niagara of the Poconos." Bushkill Creek, a tributary of the Delaware River, forms eight consecutive falls here. The private owners have erected flights of stairs to ease viewers' way around the falls. (M.C.H.A. photograph.)

Another of the Poconos' lovely falls is Eureka, near the village of Delaware Water Gap. (M.C.H.A. photograph.)

Some falls, like Indian Ladders near Canadensis, descend in stages, forming pretty little pools as they spill over rock ledges. (M.C.H.A. photograph.)

Swiftwater Falls is not high, but it presents an attractive view as its stream swirls among the rocks. (M.C.H.A. photograph.)

The Delaware River and its tributaries brought many fishermen—and women—to enjoy the beauties of streams and falls in the 1800s and early 1900s. A practical woman would wear waders in the 1930s. (Barrett Friendly Library photograph.)

One of the major pleasures of nineteenth-century summer visitors' was simply strolling down a woodland path along the river, a stream, or a lake. (M.C.H.A. photograph.)

Walking in the woods with a friend was a favorite activity in the 1930s, as it still is today. (Barrett Friendly Library photograph.)

William Brodhead, then owner of the Kittatinny House, in 1858 helped organize the Sappers and Miners Club which laid out many early trails on Mount Minsi. Members built guard rails such as this one at Caldeno Falls. (M.C.H.A. photograph.)

Childs' Arbor was named for George W. Childs, who started the Minsi Pioneers, a mountain climbing club, in 1875. Its members contributed to the safety and comfort of summer visitors by building arbors, bridges, and stairways. (M.C.H.A. photograph.)

The Mountain View Trolley was opened on July 10, 1907, as a link between Delaware Water Gap and Stroudsburg. In winter it served as a school bus; students paid 15¢ each way to attend Stroudsburg High School. (M.C.H.A. photograph.)

The summer visitors missed seeing the beauties of the Poconos in winter, such as this icy stream, but soon winter sports were developed to bring vacationers year round. (Barrett Friendly Library photograph.)

Lovely Cherry Valley, south of Delaware Water Gap, was made even more scenic by the presence of Cherry Valley Methodist Church. A horse-drawn carriage or trolley might have brought visitors to see the valley. (M.C.H.A. photograph.)

Cherry Valley's main claim to fame was the "Giant's Foot" formed by Cherry Creek's meanderings. Eventually the creek eliminated the profitable oddity by taking a shortcut across the "ankle." (M.C.H.A. photograph.)

When resorts such as the Inn at Buck Hill Falls started offering skiing and skating to winter visitors, the Lackawanna Railroad became the major conduit for customers. They disembarked at Cresco station in the mountains. (Barrett Friendly Library photograph.)

Religion as well as beautiful scenery and sports drew people to the Poconos in the 1800s and early 1900s. Here a revival meeting draws a crowd to Stroudsburg. Several resorts and camps were built as retreats by sects. (M.C.H.A. photograph.)

A mixed blessing, the Delaware and its tributaries have flooded in the past: in 1920 (above), and worst of all in 1955, when seventy people were left dead in the wake of Hurricane Diane. Dams were eventually built to prevent such tragedies. (M.C.H.A. photograph.)

But most visitors to the Poconos recall only the tranquil moods of the river and its mountains, its woodlands, and its meadows, which are what they have come here primarily to enjoy. (Barrett Friendly Library photograph.)

Two
Delaware Water Gap

The trolley terminal and Hauser's souvenir store in the center of the village of Delaware Water Gap were meeting places for summer visitors—one of whom drove the sporty little race-about car parked here. Visitors swarmed through the streets of Delaware Water Gap every summer from the mid-1800s to the 1930s. In 1906, an advertising pamphlet estimated that over a half million people visited the Delaware Water Gap and Pocono area annually. Today the borough attracts crowds for its annual summer jazz festival, the Celebration of the Arts. (M.C.H.A. photograph.)

The small village of Delaware Water Gap spread itself over the mountainside when this postcard view was made in the 1800s. Its population of 400 could accommodate 2,500 summer visitors at the height of its resort period. (M.C.H.A. photograph.)

Waiting for the mail at the post office, summer visitors had a chance to exchange experiences and meet the local residents in Delaware Water Gap. (M.C.H.A. photograph.)

Another famous postcard view of the Water Gap was this one including the Promontory. In 1909 a guide book said of the Delaware Water Gap area that "its quota of hotels is second to none in the United States." (M.C.H.A. photograph.)

Nobody seemed to mind the muddy roads as they took their daily stroll in the mountains around Delaware Water Gap. (M.C.H.A. photograph.)

At the turn of the century, a two-wheeled cart was parked along Main Street in Delaware Water Gap, where modern cars are parked today. (M.C.H.A. photograph.)

Resort hotels, small and large, lined the streets of Delaware Water Gap and could be evaluated by visitors wandering through the village, deciding where to stay on their next vacation. But most returned to a favorite hotel. (M.C.H.A. photograph.)

Hauser's wasn't the only store in Delaware Water Gap to sell souvenirs. This corner took its name from the souvenirs sold in the building at left, where the long-skirted ladies in front of it may have just made their selections. (M.C.H.A. photograph.)

Castle Inn and its music hall's most memorable moment came when John Phillip Sousa's band played there on August 20, 1912, to an audience of 875 people. Later the inn became the headquarters of Fred Waring Enterprises. (M.C.H.A. photograph.)

This Delaware Water Gap resort, the Central House, still stands. Today it houses the Deer Head Inn, a restaurant/bar which is a mecca for lovers of live jazz. (M.C.H.A. photograph.)

In 1910 a map of the village of Delaware Water Gap listed twenty-eight major resort hotels. Delaware House was one of them. (M.C.H.A. photograph.)

A. Bush was proprietor of Brodhead's Cottage, a resort on Main Street in Delaware Water Gap in 1901. (M.C.H.A. photograph.)

The Delawanna Inn in Delaware Water Gap called itself "The Little Inn Around The Corner" in 1910 because it was just off Main Street. The Stroudsburg and Water Gap trolley ran past it. (M.C.H.A. photograph.)

One of several Pocono Mountain golf courses that drew visitors was located in the village of Delaware Water Gap. (M.C.H.A. photograph.)

The serene beauty of Lake Lenape offered vacationers hiking and boating pleasure close to the Gap. Swimming also was available nearby, from a beach in the Delaware River. (M.C.H.A. photograph.)

The Delaware Water Gap Methodist Church. For the local people as well as visitors, religion was important; and churches—as they are today—were central gathering places. (M.C.H.A. photograph.)

The Delaware Water Gap villagers welcomed religious tent meetings such as this one, held on the edge of town in the early 1900s. (M.C.H.A. photograph.)

Cherry Creek Bridge, Delaware Water Gap. People who came as summer visitors and fell in love with the little village sometimes ended up moving to the area to spend their declining years, just as they do today. (M.C.H.A. photograph.)

The view from Cherry Creek Bridge. A photographer named Joseph H. Graves took this and many other postcard pictures in the village and elsewhere in the Poconos which helped make the area familiar to residents in the east. (M.C.H.A. photograph.)

Three
The Resorts

Almost as memorable as the day when John Philip Sousa's band played in Delaware Water Gap was the visit of U.S. President Theodore Roosevelt on August 2, 1910. He stayed at the Water Gap House, which overlooked the river and rivaled the Kittatinny House in size and splendor when it opened in 1872. Roosevelt had finished his second term in office in March 1909, and had made a big game hunting trip to Africa before beginning the tour of the country which brought him to Delaware Water Gap. The Gap was listed in some guide books then as one of the United States's fifteen scenic marvels. (M.C.H.A. photograph.)

The Mountain House was opened in 1871 by Theodore Hauser, a descendent of an early settler, Ulrich Hauser. The resort burned in 1987. Destruction by fire was the fate of many Pocono resorts. (M.C.H.A. photograph.)

Advertisements such as this one for the Mountain House and those for other Pocono resort hotels were carried in New York City newspapers and were successful in drawing crowds of summer visitors to the area. (M.C.H.A. photograph.)

The Kittatinny House maintained its stature among the resort hotels by hosting such attention-getting events as a dinner for Elsa Beamish, princess of the Poconos' first Laurel Blossom Festival in 1931. The annual festival continued through the 1960s. (M.C.H.A. photograph.)

Seeing and being seen by other summer visitors was important to vacationers such as these who gathered on the porch of the Water Gap House. (M.C.H.A. photograph.)

River Farm House, once a tavern and stage stop operated by Ulrich Hauser near Delaware Water Gap, was expanded into a resort hotel in 1879 by Evan Croasdale. (M.C.H.A. photograph.)

Cows roamed through the River Farm House's orchard. The resort burned down in the 1930s. It was rebuilt in the 1960s and used thereafter as a private residence. (M.C.H.A. photograph.)

The Glenwood House still stands. It was a boys' academy run by the Reverend Horatio S. Howell, but was converted to a resort hotel in 1862 after Reverend Howell died on the first day of the Battle of Gettysburg. (M.C.H.A. photograph.)

Nearby towns were quick to compete with Delaware Water Gap for the resort hotel trade. Prospect House was in East Stroudsburg. Its site is now a Baptist Church parking lot. (M.C.H.A. photograph.)

Liberty House was another early resort in East Stroudsburg. Like many of the other small resorts, its owner simply opened his home to summer visitors and advertised the fact. (M.C.H.A. photograph.)

The Indian Queen, on the other hand, was built as a hotel at 814 Main Street, Stroudsburg. It was torn down in 1963 and a bank now stands in its place. The first automobile to visit the Poconos stopped here on August 23, 1899. (M.C.H.A. photograph.)

Tannersville Inn, northwest of Stroudsburg, still stands. It now houses a popular restaurant called The Inn at Tannersville. The Pocono area phone book today lists seventy-six resorts, including the venerable Pocono Manor; but Tannersville Inn is no longer one of them. (M.C.H.A. photograph.)

Northeast of Stroudsburg was the Marshall's Falls House in the town of Marshall's Creek. Spreading trees made it a lovely place to visit. (M.C.H.A. photograph.)

Dr. William Hay, nutritionist and dietitian, owned and ran the former Mount Pleasant House resort for a time as a sanatorium he called Pocono Haven. Later it reverted to being a hotel and night spot. (M.C.H.A. photograph.)

The Peters House was a resort located near the Delaware River in the village of Bushkill. Visitors had easy access to nearby Bushkill Falls and its pavilions. (M.C.H.A. photograph.)

The Inn at Buck Hill Falls was started by a Quaker family named Jenkins. A major resort, it was near the Cresco railroad station and was one of the first to feature winter sports. It has fallen into disrepair today. (Barrett Friendly Library photograph.)

An alternative to staying at one of the big resort hotels—or a smaller one—was to rent a cottage such as this one at Buck Hill Falls, where one could do light house-keeping. (Barrett Friendly Library photograph.)

Spruce Cabin Inn at Canadensis also could be reached by way of the Lackawanna Railroad and its Cresco station. The inn is still in operation. (M.C.H.A. photograph.)

Still a very elegant resort today is Skytop, near Canadensis. It was established in reaction to the Inn at Buck Hill Falls, which allowed no drinking and no Sunday dancing. Skytop allowed both, and was a swinging resort for the younger crowd. Dog sledding was an early activity it offered. (Mary Ann Miller photograph.)

Four
Getting There

The Delaware Water Gap railroad station. The establishment of the Delaware, Lackawanna and Western Railroad on March 11, 1853, marked a sizable spurt in the growth of the Pocono Mountain resort industry. On January 21, 1856, the first train ran from Scranton, Pennsylvania, to the Delaware River, 5 miles below the Gap. By May of that year, trains went all the way to Elizabethport, New Jersey. A train leaving Elizabethport at 7:30 a.m. arrived at the Delaware Water Gap station at 1:15 p.m. Passengers would be met by surreys or, later, limousines, which took them to the resorts. (M.C.H.A. photograph.)

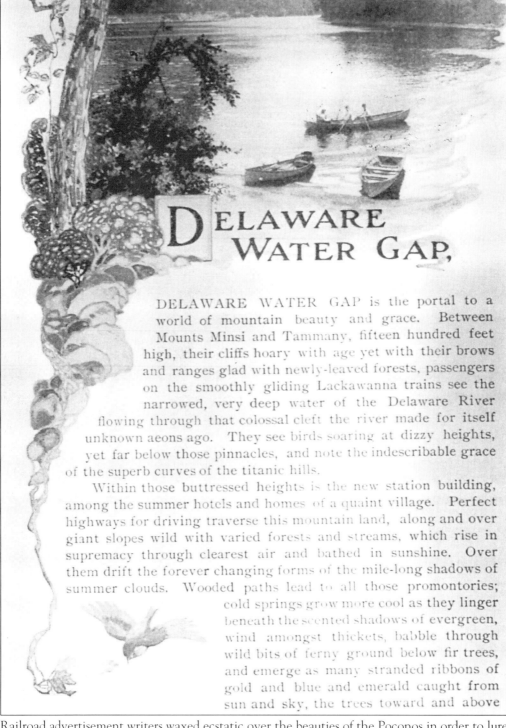

Railroad advertisement writers waxed ecstatic over the beauties of the Poconos in order to lure New Yorkers to board the Lackawanna trains to Delaware Water Gap. Here is page one of a two-page advertisement; the rest is lost, but this conveys the idea. (M.C.H.A. photograph.)

The Delaware, Lackawanna and Western station in East Stroudsburg, which served the whole Stroudsburg area, contributed to the growth of East Stroudsburg. The station is now a restaurant called Dansbury Depot. (M.C.H.A. photograph.)

The Cresco station on the Lackawanna line brought passengers to the high Poconos in both summer and winter after enterprising hotels developed winter sports and advertised them in the New York newspapers. (Mary Ann Miller photograph.)

A Lackawanna passenger train crosses Bell's Bridge over Brodhead's Creek in the Minisink Hills. The Analomink Paper Mill is at right. (M.C.H.A. photograph.)

The trains provided comfortable, dependable transportation, with Phoebe Snow advertisements attesting to the cleanliness of anthracite coal as fuel. But there was the occasional disaster, such as this wreck near Analomink in 1910. (M.C.H.A. photograph.)

When it came time for the Wilkes Barre and Eastern Railroad, another link in the rail system, to retire its last engine on December 4, 1938, there was no joy in Stroudsburg. Townspeople gathered to give it a last farewell. (M.C.H.A. photograph.)

From the early days of the Kittatinny House, its steam launch transported summer visitors on jaunts along the Delaware River. Here it pulls in at the boat landing near Delaware Water Gap. (M.C.H.A. photograph.)

Crossing the Delaware was done by ferry in the 1800s, when horses provided the transportation on dirt roads to the Gap and beyond it. (M.C.H.A. photograph.)

Before the construction of bridges across the Delaware, cars, too, had to use the ferry to reach the Pocono resort country. (M.C.H.A. photograph.)

As the twentieth century moved on into the automobile age, a horse and buggy made riding to a resort from the railroad station part of the fun of being in the Poconos. (Barrett Friendly Library photograph.)

Even more fun to ride in than a buggy was the Sleighbus, a special treat provided by the Inn at Buck Hill Falls, where skiing quickly became popular, forecasting today's busy ski scene. (Barrett Friendly Library photograph.)

By the 1920s and 1930s, resort customers were as likely to arrive by car as by train, as this Kittatinny House parking lot scene attests. But by then the railroad had done its work of familiarizing eastern urbanites with the pleasures awaiting them in the Poconos. (M.C.H.A. photograph.)

Five
Stroudsburg

Stroudsburg during the Civil War (note little girls' hoop skirts) was a busy place despite its unpaved streets. The building at left on the Main Street was the office of Dr. A. Reeves Jackson; standing in front of it is Stephen Holmes. The second building was Hollinshead Drug Store; Kresge-LeBar Drugstore, at 630 Main, is there today. The next building was the law office of Samuel S. Dreher, later president judge of Monroe County courts. In the carriage at right are John Stokes (driving) and his sister, Maria Stokes. Stroudsburg had come a long way since it was founded by Jacob Stroud nearly a hundred years earlier. (M.C.H.A. photograph.)

Fort Hamilton, in what is now Stroudsburg, was one of four area forts built to protect early settlers from frequent attacks by Minisink area Indians, who resented a trick by William Penn's son Thomas—the Walking Purchase of 1737—which they felt cheated them out of a large parcel of land. (M.C.H.A. photograph.)

Jacob Stroud built this house on Main Street for his eldest son, John, although another son, Daniel, ended up living there because John preferred to farm. Today the house, minus its porch, is Stroud Mansion, a museum and home of the Monroe County Historical Association. (M.C.H.A. photograph.)

A view of Stroudsburg showing its relationship to the Pocono Mountains was a popular postcard in the 1890s. (M.C.H.A. photograph.)

The unpaved streets of Stroudsburg made for muddy travel in wet weather. Main Street was originally named Elizabeth Street, both for Jacob Stroud's wife and for one of his daughters. (M.C.H.A. photograph.)

A trolley once crossed and recrossed the State Interborough Bridge which connects Stroudsburg with its "twin" city, East Stroudsburg. (M.C.H.A. photograph.)

Stroudsburg, the Monroe County seat, has a stone courthouse built on land donated by Jacob Stroud's grandson, Stroud Jacob Hollinshead. (M.C.H.A. photograph.)

Ducks frequented the pond at Monroe County Fairgrounds, which were located where Stroudsburg High School now stands on West Main Street. The school was built in 1929. (M.C.H.A. photograph.)

Brown and Keller sold furniture in Stroudsburg, and also served the community as undertakers. The company's hearse is at right. (M.C.H.A. photograph.)

The Penn-Stroud Hotel was built at 700 Main Street in 1833 by Stroud J. Hollinshead, who called it the Stroudsburg House, and who kept a tavern there for thirty-five years. (M.C.H.A. photograph.)

Jacob Kintz (jobber) had his business on Main Street, Stroudsburg, in 1900. On the steps are, from left to right, Evan Kintz, Howard Stofflett, Frank Spragle, and John A. Sandt. (M.C.H.A. photograph.)

The DeYoung grocery store was at the northwest corner of 8th and Main Streets in Stroudsburg. Outdoor fruit and vegetable displays attracted customers. (M.C.H.A. photograph.)

A cutter and pair stops before the stately home of Stogsdell Stokes, who, with Jacob Stroud's son, Daniel, was responsible for building the first County building in Stroudsburg. (M.C.H.A. photograph.)

Simon Meixell and his family lived in this elaborate home in the 1890s when derbies and beards were in style for men. (M.C.H.A. photograph.)

More Victorian homes lined Thomas Street. Several Stroudsburg streets, including Thomas, were named at an early date for Stroud family members. (M.C.H.A. photograph.)

A horse-drawn trolley transported Stroudsburg residents and summer guests around town in the nineteenth century. The sign advertises a program to be held in the Presbyterian church. (M.C.H.A. photograph.)

A trolley bustles along on its way to Stroudsburg's County fairgrounds on West Main Street. Livestock judging and housewives' baked goods contests were part of the annual fair run by the Monroe County Agricultural Society. (M.C.H.A. photograph.)

Six
East Stroudsburg

The East Stroudsburg railroad station. The town was originally called Dansbury for its founder, Daniel Brodhead, who in 1737 settled on land above Analomink Creek where Pocono Medical Center now stands. It was the arrival of the Lackawanna Railroad line in 1856 that caused the village to be known as "East Stroudsburg by the railroad." When it was incorporated as East Stroudsburg in 1870, the town had a population of just over five hundred. It also had its share of bed and breakfasts, rooming houses, hotels, and resorts to accommodate the summer visitors brought by the railroad. (M.C.H.A. photograph.)

A bird's-eye view of Stroudsburg was deemed just the ticket by many summer visitors for a postcard to send back to friends in the east. (M.C.H.A. photograph.)

Another view of East Stroudsburg, this one taken from an airplane, shows the village as a sprawling array of houses bordered by the railroad yards. (M.C.H.A. photograph.)

Trolley tracks speak silently of the horse-drawn trolley that once rumbled along, bell clanging, carrying its passengers down Washington Street in East Stroudsburg. (M.C.H.A. photograph.)

An early photographer produced this interesting picture of the interior of a home in East Stroudsburg at the turn of the century. The names of its subjects have been lost in time. (M.C.H.A. photograph.)

The State Normal School in East Stroudsburg was a favorite subject for postcards in the early 1900s. Its students were preparing to become teachers. (M.C.H.A. photograph.)

Another view of the Normal School was taken in 1918. Today the school is called East Stroudsburg University, and its students have a choice of many fields besides teaching. (M.C.H.A. photograph.)

The State Normal School's Zimbar Gymnasium was dedicated in 1937. School officials and community leaders came out to take part in the ceremony. (M.C.H.A. photograph.)

The American Legion Hall in East Stroudsburg was built to last as a three-story brick building with a broad front porch. (M.C.H.A. photograph.)

The predecessor of today's Pocono Medical Center was the General Hospital at 706 E. Brown Street, East Stroudsburg. Later it was called the General Hospital of Monroe County, and still later the Pocono Hospital. (M.C.H.A. photograph.)

An early private room in the hospital had spartan furnishings, but a colorful rug brightened it. (M.C.H.A. photograph.)

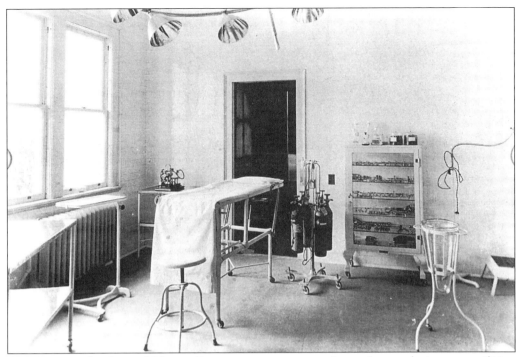
Equipment in the General Hospital's operating room was a far cry from today's rooms utilizing technological advancements. (M.C.H.A. photograph.)

The General Hospital's ambulance, photographed in 1923. (M.C.H.A. photograph.)

In 1904 the Commonwealth of Pennsylvania built the Interborough Bridge across Brodhead's Creek which separates East Stroudsburg from Stroudsburg. (M.C.H.A. photograph.)

Sturdy middle-class homes with wide porches were built along Washington Street in East Stroudsburg in the early 1900s. (M.C.H.A. photograph.)

An early place of worship in East Stroudsburg was St. Matthew's Catholic Church. Its simple design was typical of American pioneer architecture for schools as well as churches. (M.C.H.A. photograph.)

The Presbyterian Church of East Stroudsburg, on Analomink Street, burned down in 1969 and was rebuilt on the site of the Peters farm on Smith Street.. (M.C.H.A. photograph.)

Sunset View Farm, another resort hotel, had an East Stroudsburg address. Guests could enjoy the scenery from the swing at right. (M.C.H.A. photograph.)

The Prospect House in East Stroudsburg was run by Mrs. Charles Dearr, who advertised herself as "Proprietress for the 28th Season" when she had this postcard made. (M.C.H.A. photograph.)

Seven
The Mountain Towns

The store at Shafer's Corner in the village of Mountainhome served local residents but also was a place for tourists to buy supplies. Many small town businesses in the Poconos found it profitable to serve the summer visitors, and, later, the winter ski crowds—as, in fact, they still do. Not only food and snacks but also gasoline, craft items, clothing, art work, and souvenirs find buyers among today's visitors. Tourism in all its forms is still the major industry in the Poconos. (Mary Ann Miller photograph.)

Shawnee-on-Delaware was once a part of a 3,000-acre plot owned by the area's first permanent settler from the east, Nicholas Depui, who, with his family, operated a prosperous farm there. (M.C.H.A. photograph.)

Tobyhanna, founded as Naglesville, is the home of Tobyhanna Army Depot, a communications facility. It was used for training of ambulance and tank regiments and of an army air force service unit in World Wars I and II, respectively. (M.C.H.A. photograph.)

The first schoolhouse in Chestnuthill Township was built at Gilbert. Unlike most schools, it was designed to let the school teacher and his family live in one half of the building. Gilbert was called Pleasant Valley then. (M.C.H.A. photograph.)

Brodheadsville, also part of Chestnuthill Township, was originally called Shafers. It was the center of a Pennsylvania Dutch farming community. (M.C.H.A. photograph.)

A Lutheran association established a community for Lutherans at Paradise Falls, near Cresco. This store was part of that community. (Mary Ann Miller photograph.)

The Turn and Cook store in Bushkill was located near what is now U.S. Highway 209, which follows a onetime Lenape path called the Minsi. It led from the Philadelphia area to Esopus (now Kingston), New York. (M.C.H.A. photograph.)

Theo B. Price established a lumber and hardware business in Cresco in 1925. His granddaughter, Mary Ann Miller, and her husband, Warren, have expanded it today to include a well-stocked country crafts area where many visitors browse. (Mary Ann Miller photograph.)

Theo B. Price was a self-made man, Ms. Miller said, and invented and produced mine and props supplies before opening his Cresco store. (Mary Ann Miller photograph.)

Barrett Friendly Library still occupies this small stone building in Mountainhome. A crowd attended its dedication in 1912. (Mary Ann Miller photograph.)

Hotel Rapids in Analomink was a favorite hotel for fishermen, to whom it offered good food, inexpensive lodging, and superior trout fishing in nearby Brodhead's Creek. Partially destroyed by fire and flood, it houses a bar now. (M.C.H.A. photograph.)

The Luther Slutter family's homestead in Bartonsville burned around 1905. Slutter ran a sawmill which also burned some five years later. He concentrated on farming thereafter. (Frank Herting photograph.)

After the Slutter homestead burned, Luther's son Oscar bought the 119-acre farm and home of Judge Theodore Metzgar nearby. The house, on Franz Road near Ramble Bush Road in Bartonsville, today is the home of Oscar's great grandson, Paul Anderson. (Frank Herting photograph.)

Greenleaf Library was established on the grounds of the Inn at Buck Hill Falls for the use of its guests. The Inn dates from 1901. (Barrett Friendly Library photograph.)

The interior of Greenleaf Library was a cozy place to read and browse. It was lit by oil lamps which stood on tables and hung from the ceiling. (Barrett Friendly Library photograph.)

Charles F. Jenkins, operator of the luxurious Inn at Buck Hill Falls, built Griscom Lodge for some of his Quaker brethren who preferred a less expensive vacation spot where they could cook and do maintenance. (Barrett Friendly Library photograph.)

Sam Griscom originally owned the land where the Inn at Buck Hill Falls stands. He and his six brothers and five sisters posed patiently for this early photograph soon after the Civil War, when such projects took time. (Barrett Friendly Library photograph.)

Small country resorts such as Brookside Farm at Henryville abounded in the Poconos. During the Depression, many farmers sought paying guests, sending their children to sleep in the hayloft, if necessary. (M.C.H.A. photograph.)

Perhaps the most delightful of the accommodations offered by the mountain resorts were cabins in the woods where mountain laurel bloomed in early summer. (Barrett Friendly Library photograph.)

Eight
Growing Up in the Poconos

The first graders of the Delaware Water Gap School in 1949 were a bright-eyed bunch, eager to learn more about their world. And a beautiful world it was, for children growing up in the Poconos. There were trees to climb, and streams to explore, and beaches for swimming on rivers and lakes. The mountains, so foreign to the children of summer visitors, were their own familiar back yard. The Delaware Water Gap School is now the Antoine Dutot School & Museum. (Antoine Dutot School & Museum photograph.)

If you were born and raised on a Swiftwater farm, your father might let you drive his farm cart—at least as long as he held onto the horse's bridle. (M.C.H.A. photograph.)

Better yet, you might be boosted up for a ride on a work horse's back, like Kathryn Slutter was on this occasion near her Bartonsville home. But you were warned to hang on tight. (Frank Herting photograph.)

If you lived in New York City, you saw the Pocono area through the eyes of a summer visitor, and the contrast between city and country scenes made it an even more magical place. (M.C.H.A. photograph.)

Both local and visiting children could attend Pocono Pines Camp and share its fun, such as creating handicraft items in the real log cabin built around 1924 by students and instructors. (M.C.H.A. photograph.)

In the wintertime, the snow-covered mountains made sledding an exciting adventure, especially when you shared a sled with a friend. (Barrett Friendly Library photograph.)

And it was even more fun if you could slide down a snowy hillside clinging tightly to your mother's back. (Barrett Friendly Library photograph.)

The delights of skating on a frozen pond could also be shared with your parents in winter. (Barrett Friendly Library photograph.)

Even the springtime mud had its pleasures, as this boy on Franz Road in Bartonsville knew. There was less traffic to threaten you in those years. (Frank Herting photograph.)

Fishing in a mountain stream was one of the pure joys of a boy's life. And an appreciative audience could add spice to the event. (Barrett Friendly Library photograph.)

You learned the ins and outs of fishing early when you grew up in an area where trout streams abound. (Barrett Friendly Library photograph.)

Bill Rapp, who grew up to be a recognized artist, came to play at the Slutter home in Bartonsville one summer. (Frank Herting photograph.)

Visitors could spend all their time playing, but local children had chores. Some were fun, like transporting milk cans in your pony cart. (Barrett Friendly Library photograph.)

From the beginning, there was school. In Stroudsburg, these 1892 first graders had a teacher beloved throughout her working lifetime: Miss Lillie Bittenbender (right). (M.C.H.A. photograph.)

High school graduation meant the end of school days for many. But in 1925 these Stroudsburg seniors had the State Normal School at hand, just across Brodhead's Creek; and Penn State wasn't so far away. (M.C.H.A. photograph.)

If you lived in the more sparsely settled high mountains, you might have had the fun of going to this one-room school in Mountainhome. (Mary Ann Miller photograph.)

In a later year, this group of Mountainhome Grammar School students made birdhouses as a class nature study project. (Mary Ann Miller photograph.)

At Buck Hill Falls Camp Club, visiting children could meet each other at a rhythm band session. Getting acquainted was scary, but it didn't take long. You'd soon be friends. (Barrett Friendly Library photograph.)

Whatever you did all year round, from fishing to sledding to Maypole dancing at Stroudsburg's Ramsey School, you were certain to have fun growing up in the Poconos. (M.C.H.A. photograph.)

Nine
Making a Living

With tourism as the area's major industry, the Poconos offered a variety of jobs for young people. One which was especially attractive was a spot on the swimming staff at a big resort like the Inn at Buck Hill Falls. Other resort jobs for young people could involve waiting tables, carrying luggage, making beds, caring for landscaping, or polishing cars. It wasn't always easy to be the ones who were working while others were on vacation, but getting a salary was pleasant, just as it is today. (Barrett Friendly Library photograph.)

In 1888, the resort industry was reaching its height, but farming still provided a living for most northeastern Pennsylvanians, like the owners of Sunnyside Farm. (M.C.H.A. photograph.)

Haying was a weighty job for Martin Van Buren Walters (right). Children like Edward Croop helped too (the man atop the load is unknown). (M.C.H.A. photograph.)

Another major industry in the Poconos which predated the resorts was logging. Trees transported to Easton or Philadelphia on the Delaware River were tied together as rafts. (M.C.H.A. photograph.)

The Slutter sawmill in Bartonsville was a busy place, but Margery and Kathryn Slutter, daughters of the owners, could play while the grownups worked. The mill was near the present site of the Holiday Inn on Highway 611. (Frank Herting photograph.)

In 1918 horses still provided much farm power and transportation, and the blacksmith was still an important figure in the community. (M.C.H.A. photograph.)

Casper Buck's elegant hearse was pulled by horses. Buck's undertaking establishment was located in Mountainhome. (Mary Ann Miller photograph.)

The East Stroudsburg Glass Works meant jobs for many in 1893—not only men, but also young boys. Putting children to work was not looked on as exploitation then; they were used to working long hours on the family farms. (M.C.H.A. photograph.)

The Analomink Paper Mill, a thriving industrial plant, was partly destroyed by the 1955 flood. The road in background parallels today's U.S. Highway 80. (M.C.H.A. photograph.)

Ice harvesting. The eastern cities needed ice to keep food fresh, and the Poconos had lakes and ponds which made it. The railroads provided the transportation. This plant operated in Tobyhanna in 1908. (M.C.H.A. photograph.)

Joe Martocello got to have his picture taken in front of a Coolerator ice box with the crew of Stroudsburg Ice Plant because he was the boss's son. His father, Tony Martocello, is at left front. By this time, ice was made artificially. (M.C.H.A. photograph.)

M.M.T.W. Oplinger was foreman of the crew which rebuilt the first engine in the Wilkes Barre and Eastern Railroad Shops in Stroudsburg in 1894. The engine was owned by the New York Susquehanna & Western Railroad. (M.C.H.A. photograph.)

A place for women as well as men to get a job in the 1930s, when jobs were hard to find, was Mammoth Hosiery Mill, Stroudsburg. (M.C.H.A. photograph.)

Pipher's Bakery employees posed casually with their delivery truck and horse-drawn wagon. The bakery was located where Bailey's Restaurant now stands in Stroudsburg. (M.C.H.A. photograph.)

Seguine's store in Cresco, later a department store, had a staff of eight when this picture was taken. Glass cases held everything from ribbons to peanuts. (Mary Ann Miller photograph.)

Vegetables and fruits were displayed in open crates and baskets in Witte's Fish Market at 13 S. 7th Street, Stroudsburg, in 1924. John A. and Mary Witte were proprietors. (M.C.H.A. photograph.)

Fred L. Scheller's vegetable market was located at the northwest corner of 8th and Main Streets, Stroudsburg. (M.C.H.A. photograph.)

In the early days, farm families like the Slutters of Bartonsville could save money by doing many food processing jobs at home. The Slutters clearly enjoyed making apple butter together. (Frank Herting photograph.)

In August 1936, at the height of the Depression when jobs were scarce, the federal government's Works Progress Administration (WPA) paid these men to repair the roads in Stroudsburg's Courthouse Square. (M.C.H.A. photograph.)

Ten
Having Fun

The fact of the matter was that summer visitors came to the Poconos to have fun. And they were bound to do it, even though it might mean sitting on a stubborn mule looking silly while you had your picture taken. But there were many ways to have fun in the Poconos that didn't involve looking silly. You could fish or hunt, go boating or swimming, play ball games or do camp crafts, go sledding, skating, or skiing in winter, go to plays and entertainments winter or summer, or just sit and enjoy the scenery. All of these delights were available to the local residents year round. Visitors could enjoy them only briefly. (M.C.H.A. photograph.)

A rare photograph, made when photography was young, captured a moment when soldiers at a Civil War camp, in a moment of relaxation, tossed this dog high in the air from a blanket. The dog may or may not have enjoyed it. (M.C.H.A. photograph.)

Deer hunters have always enjoyed the hunting in the Poconos. Hunting has kept the deer herd at optimum size. (Frank Herting photograph.)

Fishing was also fun, as this boy's grin attests. The trout (like the deer) of the Poconos have given pleasure to sportsmen since the days of the Lenni Lenape Indians. (Barrett Friendly Library photograph.)

One man was so proud of his hour's catch on a fishing trip that he had his portrait made with it. (M.C.H.A. photograph.)

Baseball gave joy to summer visitors at a Massad Hebrew camp. No fear of strikes interrupting this game. (M.C.H.A. photograph.)

Girls at a Hebrew camp could get up their own game of basketball. There was a Massad camp at Tannersville and another at Dingman's Ferry. (M.C.H.A. photograph.)

At Summit Lake Camp, East Stroudsburg, children had fun learning to swim. Instructors were helping them develop confidence in the water in this scene. (M.C.H.A. photograph.)

Pocono Pines Camp canoeists took part in an annual water pageant on Lake Naomi. That was fun, too. Especially if you tipped over. (M.C.H.A. photograph.)

The Pocono Pines Camp crafts cabin held machine tools which boys could use to make treasures such as model airplanes and birdhouses to take home when the camp session was over. (M.C.H.A. photograph.)

Children enrolled in the Buck Hill Falls Camp Club needed only a jungle jim and each other to enjoy themselves thoroughly. (Barrett Friendly Library photograph.)

Grownups and children alike loved to play in the snow in the Poconos—and of course they still do. (Barrett Friendly Library photograph.)

Playing "crack the whip" on a frozen pond in the mountains was lots of fun for all, even when you were the one who skidded across the ice on your bottom. (Barrett Friendly Library photograph.)

Local entertainment which visitors could experience included amateur theatricals such as *Our Town*, presented by the Buck Hill Players. Leads were Patricia Johnson and Donald J. Straub. (Barrett Friendly Library photograph.)

Summer guests took part in the play *Little Lady Dresden* in an early Fourth of July celebration at the Inn at Buck Hill Falls. (Barrett Friendly Library photograph.)

Violet Clark Eddy entertained not only in the Poconos, where she lived, but also around the country with her one-woman shows involving masks. (Barrett Friendly Library photograph.)

This carriage parade could have been an event thought up by a resort recreation director—or it could have been a wedding. Whatever the occasion, it's sure to have been fun. (M.C.H.A. photograph.)

Everyone had a good time at the annual Buck Hill fair, where there was always lots to see and do with friends and neighbors, as well as the summer visitors. (Mary Ann Miller photograph.)

And sometimes it was fun just to sit by a stream like McMichael's Creek and enjoy the sunshine dancing on the water on a pleasant summer day. (M.C.H.A. photograph.)

Eleven
The Music Makers

A nationally famous musical organization, Fred Waring and his Pennsylvanians, based its operations in the Poconos and broadcast its radio shows from Worthington Hall, Shawnee, where Shawnee Playhouse is today. Waring recalled the "banjo orchestra" of his youth in a radio show he called How It All Began. Many local young people began musical careers by attending his Summer Music Workshop in Castle Inn Music Hall, Delaware Water Gap, where his Shawnee Press music publishing business also was located. He and his wife, Virginia, owned Shawnee Inn, the "Golf Capitol of the East," and had a home nearby, where Virginia, now widowed, still lives. (M.C.H.A. photograph.)

In 1933, Waring's orchestra performed regularly on radio's *Old Gold Hour*, sponsored by a cigarette company. (M.C.H.A. photograph.)

Waring's Pennsylvanians included a full-scale chorus by 1944. They made many popular recordings. Here they play the Roxy Theater in New York City. (M.C.H.A. photograph.)

Publicity shots made for Fred Waring included this one through the dramatic angle of the raised top of the grand piano, which shows him directing his brass section. (M.C.H.A. photograph.)

Rosemary Lane, Babs Ryan, and Priscilla Lane sang as a trio with Waring's orchestra in the 1930s. The Lane sisters later appeared in movies. (M.C.H.A. photograph.)

Waring featured many small groups with his orchestra. One of them was the piano duo, Cronister and Hornebrook. (Barrett Friendly Library photograph.)

Many Waring regulars, such as Leonard Kranendonk, baritone, made their homes in the Poconos. A native of Holland, Kranendonk owned a farm near Shawnee and was a local favorite who did many guest appearances in the area. (Barrett Friendly Library photograph.)

Patti Beems and Bob Sands sang romantic duets with the Pennsylvanians. (Barrett Friendly Library photograph.)

Ethel Dean West was a performing harpist in the area who predated Waring. She lived in Florida in her later years. (M.C.H.A. photograph.)

Waring's musical group was not the first to travel from the Poconos to perform. The East Stroudsburg military band played in Hagerstown, Maryland, in 1908. (M.C.H.A. photograph.)

Glenwood Hall, a Tannersville boarding house, had its own brass band in the late nineteenth century. Many local communities and groups such as the Elks had their own bands. They all added to the festivity of Fourth of July celebrations. (M.C.H.A. photograph.)

Wyckoff's Boys Club Band, sponsored by a Stroudsburg department store, was a familiar sight in the 1930s in their capes and caps. The store also sponsored a girls' harmonica band. (M.C.H.A. photograph.)

The Pocono Pines Camp lodge often bounced to the beat of a pickup jazz group. This one performed for a handful of campers in 1941. (M.C.H.A. photograph.)

Burney Whitman led a local "big band" in 1940. There was no dearth of places for Pocono musical groups to play for visitors if they were at all proficient. Every big resort offered music. (M.C.H.A. photograph.)

A top attraction at Castle Inn Music Hall in 1920 was the Jazz Phiends: Don Schiffer (drums), Walt Dreher (violin), Andy Mansfield (piano), Claude Walton (banjo), Cliff Heller (xylophone), and Russell Williams (sax). Jazz is still "big" in the Poconos today. (M.C.H.A. photograph.)

Twelve
The Great Outdoors

Among the famous people who were drawn to the Poconos to enjoy the great outdoors were the young Fred Astaire and his sister and first dance partner, Adele. They may have been guest artists at a resort. Astaire starred in many movies—most of them musicals—in the course of his career, which began in vaudeville in 1916. Canoeing was only one of the ways visitors liked to spend time outdoors in the Poconos. Others included swimming, horseback riding, fishing and hunting, sailing, playing golf, gardening, volleyball, hiking, going on hayrides, and, in the winter, skating, sledding, skiing, and riding on a dogsled. (Antoine Dutot School & Museum photograph..)

The bathing beach in the Delaware River at Delaware Water Gap was a place where few summer visitors could resist at least sticking a toe in the water. (M.C.H.A. photograph.)

Although the Inn at Buck Hill Falls and other resorts high in the mountains were far from the Delaware River, they could still offer visitors swimming in outdoor pools. (Barrett Friendly Library photograph.)

Horseback riding was a fine way to enjoy the beauties of the Poconos. There are still many riding academies in the area. (Barrett Friendly Library photograph.)

What could be a better way to revel in the scenery than becoming part of it yourself while you were fishing? (Barrett Friendly Library photograph.)

A waterfall was a source of visual pleasure as well as of fish to this nattily-dressed sportsman. (Barrett Friendly Library photograph.)

Afternoon tea al fresco became an even more delightful experience when the setting was a canoe in the Poconos. (Barrett Friendly Library photograph.)

Among all its other pleasures, the Poconos provided space for sailing in Pocono Lake Preserve. (M.C.H.A. photograph.)

Some lovers of the great outdoors preferred to enjoy it on a golf course—specifically, in this case, the 18th green at Shawnee Country Club. (M.C.H.A. photograph.)

Golf was a popular sport in the 1930s when these young women chose it as a vacation activity. (Barrett Friendly Library photograph.)

Another ever-popular outdoor activity at resorts and camps was—as it is today—volleyball. This game was at a Massad Hebrew camp. (M.C.H.A. photograph.)

City children could get their hands in the dirt when they took part in gardening activities at a Massad Hebrew camp. (M.C.H.A. photograph.)

These pretty ice skaters made a chorus line on skates as they cavorted together on Deer Lake. (Barrett Friendly Library photograph.)

All it takes for ice skaters to be happy—besides crisp weather and smooth ice—is a shelter nearby, like this one on Deer Lake, with a fire to warm their benumbed toes. (Barrett Friendly Library photograph.)

There were not many other places where you could enjoy the outdoors from a dogsled, unless you traveled to Alaska. Harry Drennan trained championship dogsled race teams in the Poconos. (Barrett Friendly Library photograph.)

A snowy mountain under a deep blue sky meant joy to yesterday's sledders as well as to today's skiers. (Barrett Friendly Library photograph.)

How about a ride with friends on a pile of straw to while away the time in the fresh air and mountain scenery of the Poconos? This one took place at Pocono Pines. (M.C.H.A. photograph.)

Enjoying the great outdoors was a religious experience for these Pocono Pines campers at Vespers services each evening. (M.C.H.A. photograph.)

A favorite activity through the years has been walking along the mountain paths and gazing at the scenery. Whatever one chose to do—or chooses to do today—the great outdoors in the Pocono Mountains of Pennsylvania has never ceased to offer a wealth of pleasure, to local residents and to visitors alike. (Barrett Friendly Library photograph.)

Acknowledgments

As was the case with my previous book in the Old Photographs series, this book could not have been compiled through my own efforts alone. I had plenty of help, most of it from Janet Mishkin, executive director of the Monroe County Historical Society, Stroudsburg. She and her assistants put up with my repeated visits and endless questions, lugged heavy file boxes of old photographs up and down three flights of stairs for my use, and cheerfully researched every detail of the area's history that they and I felt I needed to use—all this while continuing their daily work in the midst of the havoc of the Stroud Mansion's current renovation project. They couldn't have been more gracious.

Others who spent time with me and loaned their precious photographs for color photo copying were Cindy DeLucca, librarian of Barrett Friendly Library, Mountainhome; Mary Ann Miller, proprietor with her husband, Warren, of Theo B. Price Lumber, Inc., Cresco; Frank and Barbara Herting of Bartonsville; and Marty Wilson, member of the Board of Directors of Antoine Dutot School & Museum. Thank you all for your willingness to have the old pictures in your care made available to the people of your communities in this book.

Thanks also to my husband, Arthur Freedman, for his help with my data entry and word processing. He and I have lived in East Stroudsburg's Penn Estates for three and one-half years now and have come to love the Poconos. It was a delight to delve into their past during the compilation of this book. Please forgive my errors.

References

Antoine Dutot School & Museum. 1993. *Delaware Water Gap Bicentennial 1993.* DelawareWater Gap: Antoine Dutot School & Museum.
Monroe County Commemorative Book Committee. 1986. *Monroe County Sesquicentennial: 1836-1986.* Stroudsburg: Monroe County Commemorative Book Committee.
Pocono Hospital Auxiliary. 1976. *History of Monroe County, PA: 1725–1976.* East Stroudsburg: Pocono Hospital Auxiliary.